Old KILMAURS and FENWICK

by
Alex F. Young

Although Captain Armstrong's map of Ayrshire, surveyed in 1775, does not show the tolbooth of Kilmaurs, the town house of today must have replaced its predecessor (which was built around 1604) on the corner of Irvine Vennel shortly after this date. Despite calls over the years to raze it, the tolbooth symbolises Kilmaurs. Nature, however, very nearly succeeded in August 1874, when during a thunder storm a bolt of 'electric fluid' struck the spire, bringing down the top twelve feet and its weather cock onto the steps. The only injury was to the civic purse which was drained of £84 17s. 9d. for repairs. The tolbooth was also the place of penance in times past when miscreants were chained in the Jougs, or iron neck ring, attached to the front of the building. No record of those punished in this way survives, but it is said to have last been used in 1812.

© Stenlake Publishing, 2001
First published in the United Kingdom, 2001,
by Stenlake Publishing, Ochiltree Sawmill, The Lade,
Ochiltree, Ayrshire, KA18 2NX
Telephone / Fax: 01290 423114
enquiries@stenlake.co.uk
www.stenlake.co.uk

ISBN 1 84033 150 X

FURTHER READING

The books listed below were used by the author during his research. None of them are available from Stenlake Publishing. Those interested in finding out more are advised to contact their local bookshop or reference library.
The Statistical Account of Scotland, Vol. IX, 1791–1793.
The Third Statistical Account of Scotland (Ayrshire), 1951.
The *Kilmarnock Standard*; The *Air Advertiser*; The *Ayrshire Post*.
Robert Beattie & Kilmaurs Historical Society, *Kilmaurs – Past and Present*, 1993.
George Chalmers, *Caledonia: A Historical and Topographical Account of North Britain*, 1887.
Rev. J. Kirkwood Fairley, *Matthew Fowlds and Other Fenwick Worthies*, 1910.
D. McNaught, *Kilmaurs Parish & Burgh*, 1912.
James Taylor, *Annals of Fenwick*, 1970.

ACKNOWLEDGEMENTS

The publisher wishes to thank the following for permission to reproduce the photographs in this book: Mrs J.C. McKellar of Fenwick for the front cover; Mr William Gray of Kilmaurs for page 14; Mr Frank Beattie for page 15; Robert Grieves for page 37 (left); and East Ayrshire Museums and Arts Section for those on pages 5, 7, 8, 16, 17 (both) and the back cover.

The author also thanks the following for easing the burden of his research: Ms S.C. Cockburn, Mrs B. Gaffney, Mr William Gray, Ms J. Johnstone, Mr William Millar, Mr Watson Muirhead, Ms Effie Walker, Auckland Museum (New Zealand), the Royal Mail Heritage Services, Ayrshire Archives Centre, East Ayrshire Council (Cemeteries), the Baird Institute, Cumnock, Glasgow Museum of Transport, the Dick Institute, Kilmarnock, and Carnegie Library, Ayr.

A photograph of the swing park by Fenwick Parish Church, taken while on a visit in the summer of 1960 by the Rev. George Allan who had been minister there between 1933 and 1935. The kids playing are Linda Anderson, David Young and Tom McKellar.

INTRODUCTION

No one can state with certainty the derivation of the name Kilmaurs. In the *Statistical Account* of the 1790s, the Rev. Alexander Millar ('Wee Miller' of Robert Burns's poem 'The Holy Fair') believed 'Maurs' may have been a tribute to the Virgin Mary, although he also recognised the village's connections with St Maurs. Modern thinking favours a derivation of the Gaelic *Cill mor ais* – 'the hill of the great cairn' – and certainly the village is ringed with the remnants of crannogs and hill forts.

Through the influence of Cuthbert, third Earl of Glencairn (1503–1540), James V made Kilmaurs a burgh of barony in 1527, and a parish council was set up with the right to create burgesses and elect bailies. The Earl of Glencairn, in his capacity as patron of the parish, also granted 240 acres of land for cultivation to various tradesmen, including coopers, fullers, masons, tailors and woodworkers, and the forty, six acre, plots were so productively husbanded that kale became a major earner in the parish. Over the years, the powers of the parish council diminished until by the 1950s it was left with just one responsibility – the maintenance of the tolbooth, which was where it met.

By the seventeenth century, Kilmaurs's cutlers were producing knives superior to those manufactured in either Sheffield or Birmingham. However, a century later, cheap mass production in the south sounded the death knell of this industry. In memory of their skills, there lives on the saying, *as gleg as a Kilmaurs Whittle*, i.e. 'to be as sharp as sharp.' Today, this local industry is also remembered in the name of the village's Gleg Whittle restaurant.

In the eighteenth century, cottage weavers became a major force across the country, but even with the introduction of the power loom, as at Fenwick, weaving remained a cottage industry in Kilmaurs. The last looms were not removed from Townend until 1902, when the buildings were fully converted into houses.

In 1820, within the village population of 719, there were ninety weavers and forty-two shoemakers. Although Stewarton was the 'Bonnet Town', bonnet making was also important to Kilmaurs until American and German tariff barriers crippled the industry in the 1880s.

Despite competition from its industrialised neighbour, Kilmarnock, the manufacturing of boots and textiles continued in Kilmaurs into the twentieth century. The boot manufacturer, Kellie & Co., based on Irvine Road, employed 130 until the 1920s and was succeeded in the same premises by the Carmel Hosiery Manufacturing Co. which had transferred from Kilmarnock with a workforce of 120.

Kilmaurs's most renowned son was Sir John Boyd Orr, who was born in the house Holland Green on Fenwick Road in 1880. On graduation he entered medicine, before studying animal nutrition at Aberdeen. During the First World War he served with the Royal Army Medical Corps, winning a DSC and an MC. Returning to Aberdeen University, he became Director of the Rowett Institute and Professor of Agriculture. Two of his studies, 'National Food Supply' and 'Food, Health and Income', became the foundation of the food rationing system in the Second World War. Knighted in 1935, he was later made a peer and won the Nobel Peace Prize in 1949. He died in 1971.

When 'Phinigh', 'Finnick', or Fenwick was created a separate parish from that of Kilmarnock in 1642 and given its own church (which survives, refurbished after a serious fire in 1929), its parishioners were not only relieved of the nine mile round trip to Kilmarnock every Sunday, but were also granted a parish council to manage the affairs of an area which extended nine miles east to west and six miles from north to south. Over the years the parish name changed from New Kilmarnock to Fenwick.

At that time the village (what is now Laugh or Low Fenwick) was no more than a hamlet, standing where the great road from Glasgow branched to Kilmaurs in the west and to what would later become Waterside to the east. Later, expansion north along the Glasgow road would see Townhead and High Fenwick come into being. In 1933 Fenwick's days as a staging post passed with the opening of the trunk road by-pass which runs in an arc a few hundred yards west of the village.

The new church brought development along New Road which ran east from Main Road through the glebe and Kirkton, down to Spoutmouth and the bridge over Fenwick Water.

A banner, now displayed in the church, bearing the words *Phinigh for God, Cwntry and Covenanted Work of Reformation* ('King' was omitted) bears witness to the killing times of the seventeenth century and the eight Fenwick Covenanters who gave their lives for their beliefs. James White, John Ferguson, George Woodburn and Peter Gemmell are buried in the churchyard, while Robert Buntine lies at Glasgow Cathedral, James Blackwood at Irvine and Captain John Paton, hanged in Edinburgh's Grassmarket, lies in Greyfriars churchyard. These last three are remembered with commemorative stones.

While other parts of Ayrshire developed coal mining, Fenwick relied on shoemaking, weaving and farming. Writing in the parish's entry in the *Statistical Account* of the 1790s, the Rev. William Boyd reported: 'At present, there may be in the parish 270 horses; many of them high priced; 2,000 black cattle; and, in the moor farms, 2,300 sheep.' Of the seventy-eight families in the village at this time, forty-six were supported by the weaver's loom and sixteen by the shoemaker's last.

From the shoemakers came Fenwick's most famous son, John Fulton. In 1833, with little more than the tools of his craft and ten years labour, Fulton completed an orrery, a clockwork model of the solar system named after the fourth Earl of Orrery (1676–1731) by its inventor, George Graham. This was no mean feat in the days before mechanised tools and the John Fulton Memorial Hall in Main Road (built as the Guthrie Memorial Church in 1843) stands as his monument.

In 1824 Fenwick's cottage industry of spinning and weaving entered the new century and the fringes of industrialisation when Hugh Alexander built his carding and spinning mill on Craufurdland Water at Waterside. This business, which was succeeded in the same premises by the Fenwick Farmers Co-operative Association's creamery, have been the parish's largest employers.

Looking down Main Street, Kilmaurs, towards the tolbooth, the 'Hangman's House' (nobody knows how it got this name) can just be seen against its north wall. On the left, just before the white harled Wheat Sheaf Inn, was Joe Murphy's greengrocer shop. Murphy kept a horse and cart, and there is a story about the trouble he had with the nag, which was hard of hearing. When Murphy shouted a hello to friends he was passing in the street, the horse would always stop, thinking it heard, 'Wo!'. Joe earned a reputation as a dancing master, his class of Highland dancers performing at the Empire Exhibition in Glasgow in 1938. In the centre, towards the corner of Irvine Road, the present Masonic hall has served as a billiard hall and a Hornby model railway club venue. This photograph was used on a postcard, sold by Miss Jones, the stationer, whose shop stood just behind the photographer.

Pictured outside Hugh Montgomery's blacksmith shop, which stood in Fenwick Road behind the Weston Tavern, are (left to right) David Dickson, unknown, Hugh Montgomery, Douglas Gilmour, David Mitchell, Robert Spence and James Hillhouse. Whether their business was with the blacksmith or with the tavern is not recorded. The shop could be a dangerous place when the sparks flew, but Montgomerie's philosophy to those who warmed themselves on cold days was, 'If you're no in your ain road, you're no in mine.'

When this photograph was taken, the water pump at Townhead provided the principal water supply for many villagers. As late as 1950, forty of the village's 580 houses had no internal water supply. One of these pumps has been retained as an ornament outside the library premises in Irvine Road.

While much of the east side of Main Street and Townhead has survived, the west side has been swept away and rebuilt over the years. One of the buildings in this picture which was later demolished was, jutting out on the left, the 'Barracks', a house built in the early nineteenth century by James Smith, a retired army lieutenant. A founder member of the Farmer's Society which was established around 1824, Smith kept ducks and geese in a pond fronting the house.

The Kilmaurs 'fire engine' on parade in the pageant to celebrate the Silver Jubilee of King George and Queen Mary in May 1935. On this occasion, Gilbert Murphy was the driver while Tommy Hunter and Robert Clarke manned the pump. The klaxon operator cannot be identified. The engine is said to date from 1830, but at their meeting on 5 October 1880 the town council decided that as it was irreparable, it would be disposed of and the premises (in the tolbooth's ground floor) let to a suitable tenant. Although unrecorded, it is likely that a new fire engine (the one seen here) was subsequently bought. By the 1930s it would certainly have been redundant and fire fighting services provided by Kilmarnock. By today's standards it is tiny, measuring only three metres long by 114 centimetres wide. In 1968 it was given to the Fire Brigade Museum in Edinburgh, but in March 2001 was returned to East Ayrshire Council's Museums and Arts Section who hope to put it on public display.

Also taking part in the Jubilee celebrations was Tom Fry, or 'Tossy' as he was known, pictured here mounted on the horse, Scotia II. Tom, who passed away a number of years ago but is remembered as a bit of a wag, lived at Townend with his two brothers.

Opened in 1904, the Kilmaurs branch of the Kilmarnock Equitable Co-operative Society at 5 Main Street, was photographed for the society's fiftieth anniversary book, *A Fifty Years' Record*, in 1910. The building's earliest surviving deed dates from 1820 when it was bought from the Widow Fulton by James Ralston, cornet of the 86th Regiment and later preses (or chairman) of the parish council. What had been a stable and barn, he rebuilt as a house. After the passing of the Co-op as a retail force, the premises became the Gleg Whittle coffee and craft shop in 1980 and is now a restaurant. To the right of the Co-op was John Arnott's drapery shop, while to the left is Rowallan View which for many years housed a branch of the Bank of Scotland.

From the rear of the properties on the east side of Main Street, this view from 1904 takes in Monks Well Bridge over the Carmel Water, the bowling green, and the Castle and the Place on the hill beyond. The bridge was built in 1824 and takes its name from a well or spring a few yards upstream. Bowling came to Kilmaurs in 1869 when Colonel W.P. Adam of Tour recruited thirty-five members by the sale of shares and laid a thirty by forty yard green. The club's rules carried the stipulation: 'Members guilty of spitting, swearing or other ungentlemanly conduct may be fined, and if repeated or the fine unpaid, expelled.' The membership, the green and the clubhouse have all expanded over the years. In his survey of 1608, Timothy Pont wrote 'Ye castell [of Kilmaurs] is ane ancient stronge building belonging to ye Earls of Glencairn environed with a parke called Carmel Wod . . . .' Behind the castle stands the Place, a house dating from the early seventeenth century. It may have been built by the Glencairns, but by 1793 was in the hands of Captain James Ralston. It is still used as a private residence today.

From the tolbooth in Main Street, Fenwick Road sweeps eastwards out of Kilmaurs to the A77 and Fenwick. On the right of the picture, beyond the street light standard and the barefooted boy, the buildings end at the Glencairn Church which has a long history. The congregation was founded in 1740 by the Rev. David Smyton as the Associate Congregation, having broken with the Established Church. In 1852 they built this new church on plans commissioned from the Edinburgh architects, Peddie and Kinnear. This partnership was responsible for many of the bank buildings springing up at the time, as well as Aberdeen City Hall. The final cost of the church came to £1,311 14s. 2½d. Plans to install stained glass in the large rose windows fell through when they could not be obtained at under £5 each. Following the amalgamation with St Maurs Church in 1963, the building served as a church hall until purchased in the late 1980s by the current owners, Glencairn Studio, manufacturers, ironically, of stained glass windows.

The highway from Kilmarnock entering Kilmaurs at Townend, *c*. 1904. The angle of the houses on the left shows the line of the old road to the river and the ford which was used before the building of the bridge (which was widened in 1880). This divergent road, which leads to the house Sackville, also once led to the village's gasworks which had been built in the 1820s. On the right, just before the bridge, stands the roadman's cottage. The first two storey building on the left was the manse from which the lintel stone inscribed with the words 'Walk in the light' (from Isaiah, 2. 5) was taken. When the inscription was made it was the home of the Rev. David Henderson, minister between 1589 and 1637, and the stone is now incorporated in a plinth at Catherine Place which was built on the site of the manse.

From the railway embankment, this view to the north-west extends from Yardside Road in the foreground to the mansions which sprung up on Irvine Road in the early years of the twentieth century. When John Bowie came to the forty-eight arable acres of Yardside Farm in the 1870s, he employed a man and two women to work the farm, but by 1880 the first houses were beginning to eat up his land. As an indication of the openness of the countryside to the west of Kilmaurs, the houses of the villa in the foreground are named Seaview and Arranview.

Kirkton Cottages once housed the beadle of St Maurs Church and where they once stood now serves the kirk as a parking area. There may also have been another row of cottages opposite, backing onto the church wall. Pictured here at her door is Mrs Mary Gray, who had come to Kirkton in 1911 from the Earl of Eglinton's farm, Floors, on the Stewarton Road, after her husband was killed on the railway. To the left of Mrs Gray, Mrs Jean Fleming stands with her daughter Mary and youngest son James. Setting out on his bicycle is Robert Fleming. A stable at the far end of the row served farmers' horses and gigs on Sabbath mornings.

Close by the railway bridge over Irvine Road stood the boot and shoe factory of Kellie and Co. John Kellie, a leather merchant from Minnigaff in Kirkcudbrightshire, founded the company in the late 1870s. By the time of this 1904 photograph, he and his family had moved from Kilmarnock to the house he built in Yardside. After Kellie's business closed, Tom Auld took the premises on as a hosiery in 1928 and at one point employed 130 workers before selling out to Glenlomond Fire Surrounds. They later moved to Carmelside at Townend, and following a fire, the old boot factory was demolished. The site is now occupied by The Braes housing development.

Throughout the 1880s and '90s Kellie & Co.'s business went from strength to strength, reaching its apogee during the First World War. In this photograph from that period, taken to commemorate a collection for the war effort, there are as many women operatives as journeymen shoemakers employed to produce boots for the forces. The company's failure to recognise changes in the footwear market and in manufacturing methods in the post-war period led to its decline and final closure.

Despite the loss of his right arm as a twelve year old, William Lindsay became an active sportsman. His prowess as a left-handed shooter, bowler, quoiter, curler and angler earned him the status of a local legend. In the late 1850s his father brought the family from Mauchline to the forty-eight acre arable farm of Towerhill in Kilmaurs. Despite his disability, William, on top of running the farm after his father's death in 1877, was also the Poor Law inspector of the parish for many years. On his death in 1926 he left an estate valued at £2,604 1s. 10d.

Another Kilmaurs notable, although not a native, was the herbalist William Aird, or 'Herb Willie' as he was better known. A Christadelphian, his companion on herb hunting trips was his bible. According to local legend, he was brought up on Brackenhill Farm as a herd boy and later took to weaving, when jibes about his moustache from fellow weavers brought out the poet in him: 'Ye woolen wabsters needna fash/ To meddle Poet Wull's moustache,/ It didna cost you any cash/ to put it there . . . '. However, research reveals that he was born in West Calder about 1818 and that his wife and assistant herbalist, Jean, was a native of Stranraer. While in Kilmaurs during the 1890s and early 1900s they resided in Main Street and Sunnyside.

According to Chalmers' *Caledonia*, when Kilmaurs's parish church was built in 1413 it was dedicated to St Maurs who came to the area in AD 868 and died at Kilmaurs in 887. This building replaced a previous church which dated from 1140, but the church in this photograph – the one still in use today – dates from 1888, when extensive restructuring was undertaken. In the hollow below the church sits Tour Farm, which probably has more visible history in its environs than the church as the foundations of the Vicarage Tower (or 'Tour'), from which the farm takes its name, can be seen there. The tower appears to have been a fortified building of some kind and is of unknown age, but a nearby dovecot bears the date 1636.

Although the Rev. Alexander Miller recorded in the *Statistical Account* of the 1790s that 'a disposition to secede from the Established Church hath long subsisted among the inhabitants of Kilmaurs', it was not until the Disruption of 1843 that the step was taken by four elders and 120 members of the parish church. Joining the Free Church of Scotland, they built their new church in Crosshouse Road and this was later named the Maxwell United Free Church in memory of the Rev. James Maxwell, who was the congregation's second minister, serving from 1848 until his death in 1885. Ironically, he was interred in St Maurs's churchyard.

The Glasgow, Barrhead & Kilmarnock Joint Railway reached Stewarton in 1871 and two years later, on 26 June, Kilmaurs Station also opened, giving the village a link to both Kilmarnock and Glasgow. The feats performed by the engineers who planned and built the railway system, which cut through hills and bridged chasms, must be admired. Coming from Stewarton to Kilmaurs, the line runs through a twenty-five feet cut for a distance of eight hundred yards, and south of Kilmaurs the valley of the Carmel is crossed by a viaduct of six spans of thirty feet which carries the line fifty-two feet above the river. In November 1966 the Kilmarnock–Barrhead line was closed under the Beeching Plan, but was re-opened in 1984 by Strathclyde Passenger Transport Executive. The 'dookie' under the viaduct is remembered as a popular place in summer for Kilmaurs youngsters, while the older generation of the village could stretch their legs with 'a walk roon the viaduct'.

The junction of the Glasgow road at Low Fenwick, where the left fork made for Kilmarnock and the right for Kilmaurs and Stewarton. The little row of houses at the junction stand on 'Kilmaurs Knoll' which was once part of Greenwalls Farm (now the Fenwick Hotel). They have changed little since this photograph was taken around 1912. The two storey whitewashed house at the far end (now 3 Main Road) dates from 1815. It was bought in 1855 by Fenwick Parochial Board, ' . . . for the management of the affairs of the poor . . . ', and was used as a lodging house for itinerant workers, run at that time by John Cook. In the middle of the row was Rolyat (now 15 Main Road), home of Hugh S.P. Taylor, whose initials appear on many of the photographs in this collection. A professional photographer, Taylor was a native of Glasgow, but ended his days in Fenwick in 1943 at the age of eighty. One of his daughters, possibly Jeanie, stands at the junction in her summer dress and straw hat.

H·S·P·T. — *Fenwick Motor* —

Built by Albion Motors of Scotstoun, Glasgow, this thirty-two horsepower chain driven A10 omnibus dates from around 1913 and was run by Richard Johnstone, a Fenwick carrier and coal merchant who started a regular bus service between the village and Kilmarnock. In 1914 he opened a service between Kilmarnock and Irvine. Pictured outside Hugh Taylor's house at Low Fenwick, John Cameron is at the wheel while Taylor's daughter Jeanie sits immediately behind him.

The north entrance to Hillhouse Lodge (now a nursing home) was flanked by Wee Davie Walker's cottage on the right and the village pump on the left. Known as 'Old Parliament Corner', this site witnessed many rowdy meetings when weavers were a political force during the first half of the nineteenth century. Here, sheltered from the worst of the prevalent westerly weather by the Hillhouse trees, they met in an atmosphere the authorities viewed as seditious while lookouts watched the road from Kilmarnock and the byway down Waterslap. An active member of the Weavers Society, Wee Davie addressed many of these meetings until his death in March 1851. Reduced to a metre high, the outer walls of his cottage survive as a garden feature of the adjacent house which was at one time an inn. Some years ago the pump was removed to the other side of the roadway, before it finally vanished.

The view of the interior of John Walker's cottage in Waterslap shows the centrepiece of a late nineteenth century cottage, the open fireplace. Set amongst otherwise spartan conditions, the fire burned both coal and peat. Above it, the ever simmering black kettle hung from the swee. It is likely that some time later the open fire would have been replaced with a range. Born in Fenwick around 1820, John was a wool weaver; his wife Mary was from Kilmarnock. In keeping with weaving's tradition as a cottage industry, the census of 1881 shows that the couple had a lodger, Livingstone Gibson, a twenty-eight year old wool weaver from Kilmarnock.

A local band of minstrels entertaining Miss Mary Ann Wales at the door of her spirit shop on the east side of Low Fenwick, a business she carried on for a time after the death of her father, Hugh. The musicians cannot be positively identified, but are thought to be John Wales on fiddle and Dan Brown on the penny whistle. Willie Gemmell has his cap in hand while Tam 'Lichtnin', the postman, watches from his tricycle.

When building Dunselma (known locally as the 'House on the Hill') on the grounds of Langside Farm above Low Fenwick in 1935, George B. Dunlop, proprietor of the *Kilmarnock Standard* and principal shareholder of Kilmarnock Football Club, and his wife, Dr Annie I. Dunlop, agreed that their home would eventually be gifted as an eventide home to the Church of Scotland. Following Mr Dunlop's death in October 1951, Annie stayed on for four years before relinquishing it to the Church. She was the guest of honour at the home's opening on 11 September 1957. The original accommodation for forty residents has since been reduced as day care and 'outreach' home care of the elderly has increased. Dr Dunlop died a resident of the home.

Mansheugh H.S.P.T. c 1900.

This 1900 Taylor photograph of Mansheugh (which translates as 'ditch of willows') shows it during the period of transition from thatch to slate. In the 1640s the ruined left hand end was reputedly the home of the first minister of the parish, William Guthrie, while he awaited the building of the manse. It is also remembered as the home of Jeanie Campbell during the 1930s, who used the slated end as a byre and supplied the school with its milk. In winter the children were given the choice of having it hot or cold.

In 1782, when the Rev. William Boyd was forced, against the wishes of some parishioners, on Fenwick parish by its patron, the Earl of Glasgow, the Rev. James Dewar formed the breakaway Associate or Burgher Congregation (which later became part of the United Presbyterian Church). In his poem, 'The Ordination', Robert Burns wrote of the schism: 'As lately Fenwick, sair forfairn,/ Has proven to its ruin'. Their church stood until 1831 when it was superseded by what became the Orr Memorial Free Church (with adjoining manse), named after Dewar's successor, the Rev. William Orr, who served the congregation for fifty-two years until his death in 1882. In 1843 a splinter from this congregation built the Guthrie Memorial Church (named after William Guthrie (1620–1665), the first minister of the parish), which later became and survives as the John Fulton Memorial Hall (renamed after the orrery builder), the congregation having merged back with the Orr Memorial Church. In 1933 the cycle came full circle when the parish reunited under the roof of the established Church of Scotland. The Orr Memorial Church building lingered on for some years, serving at times as a furniture store before being demolished in 1947. The manse still stands.

TOWNHEAD-FENWICK

H.S.P.T.

As in many of his photographs, Hugh Taylor featured his daughters Jeanie, here with a bicycle, and Clementina in this picture of Wee Townhead which sits on the west side of Main Road at the head of Low Fenwick. The first building on the left was John 'Millman' Watt's, who, latterly with his two sons, ran a carrier's business and also operated a steam thrashing mill at harvest time. His property survives as a house. At the end of the row, just before Langside Farm, Robert Burns stands at his door. Robert, a land drainer, lived here with his widowed mother Mary and then with his wife Janet until his death in 1931 at the age of eighty-six.

Mr David Dick (right) and his wife Jean at the rear of their cottage at Wee Townhead (22 Main Road), with two gentlemen and a cow. Born in Maybole in 1841, David was an agricultural labourer, while Jean, twelve years younger, was from Kilwinning. The couple give a good example of the itinerant lives led by nineteenth century agricultural workers as their daughters, Elizabeth, Agnes, Lillias and Margaret, were born in Kilmarnock, Dundonald, and Fenwick respectively.

Looking north along Main Road, this photograph from around 1910 shows how little Fenwick's Main Road changed throughout the twentieth century, apart from the increased dangers in crossing it! The Kings Arms Hotel has been repainted, while its competitor, the Wallace Arms, on the left beyond the John Fulton Memorial Hall, is now the village surgery. The war memorial now takes the empty site at the farthest point of the photograph. Later, the road was tarmacked, pavements were laid and street lighting, initially gas, was installed. The first house on the right, Glebe Cottage, dates from 1784 and was the home of John Gemmell, a staunch member of the Fenwick Weavers Society, who died in 1875. It now has fresh whitewash, but retains the five bar gate which once led into the adjacent field on the glebe.

The Kings Arms Hotel in Main Road probably dates from the eighteenth century and was long a busy staging post on the route south out of Glasgow, when the stagecoach could take eight hours on its journey to Ayr. At one time the hostelry catered for eight coaches and up to thirty carriers' wagons per day. The extensive stabling, which stood to the rear, gave way to a parking area many years ago. At the Venetian style window on the left, brides on their great day would cut their wedding cake and throw favours to the assembled crowd in the street below. The set of steps on the right have been taken away, as has much of the Tudor style timbering, and the entrance on the left has been modernised.

Dating from 1643, Fenwick Kirk, with its harling finish, crow step gables and Gothic windows, was the hub of village life. In his report for the *Statistical Account* of the 1790s, however, the Rev. Mr William Boyd was a little less than complimentary about it: ' . . . by far too large for the parish; and, from its not being plastered, cold and uncomfortable in winter, the snow often lying in it some inches deep.' Later, seating for four hundred was installed, but initially it had a bare earthen floor with a single row of seats around the walls. Those wishing a seat brought a stool. This photograph was taken around 1895.

In the early hours of Sunday 24 November 1929 fire broke out in Fenwick Kirk. Press reports credit the discovery of the fire to a newspaper delivery car driver who raced to Kilmarnock Fire Station to raise the alarm. Locals say Marion Rodger raised the alarm. By the time fire brigade arrived, some forty minutes later, the roof was gone and the interior destroyed. The cause was later found to have been a fault in the heating system. By February 1931, the roof had been rebuilt, the interior refurbished, and services had resumed. One little difficulty arose, however, with the slating work, which was done by Matthew Miller of Stewarton. On the east roof of the south transept, Miller set a latin cross in black slate amongst the greys, greens and blues. The Rev. Andrew Burns, who had held the charge since 1887 and would retire the following year, saw it as graffiti on a Presbyterian church, but was powerless to erase it. In the right conditions, it still stands out clearly, whereas the smaller one Miller experimented with is a little more difficult to find – good luck!

TOP OF KIRKTON BRAE.

Alexander Cuthbert outside his cottage at Kirkton Brae which stood opposite the parish church where he served as beadle and gravedigger in his later years. Born in Fenwick in 1812, 'Sanny', as he was known, was a wool weaver by trade. He remained unmarried and in his later years was cared for by his niece, Janet. His cottage, in a dilapidated condition in this photograph by Hugh Taylor taken in the 1890s, probably did not stand for much longer. An oil painting, now in possession of the church, was made from this photograph by David Robertson in August 1940. The site of the cottage is now occupied by a modern house, 23 Kirkton Road.

Taken around 1890, this photograph of Spoutmouth, looking up Kirkton Brae from the bridge over Fenwick Water, shows its inhabitants in their Sunday best. Outside the house on the left are the Montgomerys – brother and sister Robert and Jessie, with their mother Jean, then in her mid-sixties. Robert was a commercial traveller to the provision trade, while the two women were seamstresses. Beyond them stand the Cuthberts outside their home. At the house on the right, stand a group of the nephews and nieces of Fenwick's most famous son, John Fulton, who died in 1850. Born here in 1800, Fulton followed his father's trade of shoemaker and built his orrery at his workbench in the house.

It can safely be presumed that Robert Fulton, pictured chained in the Jougs on the south wall of Fenwick Church, was merely posing for this photograph and not there by order of the kirk session. According to the minutes of the kirk session from the eighteenth century, one could expect punishment by attachment to these if caught for misdemeanours such as 'brek of ye Saboth in dryveing [a] kow towards Kilmarnock on ye Lords day' and 'for being somewhat overtaking with drink'. One man was punished for 'swearing, cursing and flyting with his mother-in-law', another for the 'inhuman throwing of Elizabeth White over a brae', and another 'for cursing ye day that ever ye minister came to this countrie'. A similar 'emblem of shame' can still be seen on the wall of the tolbooth in Kilmaurs.

By the 1920s, Richard Johnstone's Fenwick based bus company was successful enough for him to invest in new buses. Here George Welsh, a driver with the company, is pictured with a newly delivered Dodge motor bus (the registration GB was used between January 1922 and July 1925). According to the destination board, the bus operated on Johnstone's original route of 1913, Fenwick to Kilmarnock.

John Fulton (standing) with his brother Robert and sisters Lizzie (left) and Janet, photographed around 1904. Nephews and nieces of the John Fulton who built the orrery in the cottage at Spoutmouth, John and the two sisters also lived in the cottage. John, who died in 1937 aged ninety-one, worked the ground between the cottage and Fenwick Water as a market garden and made a comfortable living from his strawberry crop, amongst others. Robert was also a gardener and at the time of this photograph was employed at the East Chapelton Reformatory in Bearsden. Lizzie (proper name Elizabeth Ann) was a dressmaker, while Janet worked as a seamstress. Lizzie died in 1927, aged sixty-seven, and Janet in 1931, aged seventy-seven. Both are buried with John in Fenwick Cemetery.

John Fulton with his sister Janet and Ruby the cat, photographed outside their cottage at Spoutmouth in November 1924, a few weeks after the thatch on the roof had been replaced with slate. A message on the rear of the postcard from which this picture is taken says that their sister Lizzie was away from home, staying with a Mrs P. Walker in Kilmarnock. If the Fultons were still around today, they would barely recognise Spoutmouth as their cottage has long since been demolished and replaced by modern buildings.

This family group, photographed at Langside Farm in the summer of 1906, consists (from left to right) of Agnes Cameron, her farmer husband William Cameron, their son William, daughter Mary, granddaughter Agnes Kennedy, and Annie McKellar. A lintel inscription – 'TB 1723 EB' – above the door behind them recalls the marriage of Thomas Buntine and Elizabeth Gemmel, earlier occupants of the fifty-two acre arable farm, who were wed in July 1723. Elizabeth was buried on 1 September 1762 and Thomas on 17 December 1766. Ironically, one hundred years earlier, on 19 December 1666, Robert Buntine, a Fenwick Covenantor, was executed at Glasgow for his beliefs. He lies in Fenwick churchyard. When the Camerons died the farmstead served McKellar the joiner as a wood store and is now Langside Guest House.

Harvest time at Langside Farm around 1904. A busy time, before the days of the combine harvester, when all hands were called upon. The farmer will have been leading the horse and hayrake, assisted by the boy, while his wife and the farm hand at the left of the picture built the stacks. Judging by the weather that day and the number of haystacks already made in the field beyond, the harvest had been a good one, providing ample feed for the winter ahead.

Standing at the head of Main Road, Fenwick's war memorial was dedicated on 5 June 1921 to the thirty-six men of the parish who gave their lives in the First World War. John McGill, a cousin to Johnstone the haulier, was the bugler at this ceremony. Among the names on the memorial can be found Adam McEwan, from Balgray Mill, who, as part of the Highland Light Infantry's contingent with the Egyptian Expeditionary Force, died of his wounds at Alexandria on 29 August 1917; the Rev. John C. Lambert's two sons, twenty year old William, a 2nd lieutenant in the Cameronians who ventured into no man's land on the night of 23 March 1916 to inspect the German wire defences and was caught by a German machine gunner, and twenty-five year old George who was killed in the trenches in April 1917. A further inscription bearing the names of the nine men killed in the Second World War was unveiled on 6 July 1952 by Col. M.C. Hamilton-Campbell, Depute Lieutenant of Ayrshire.

Claimed to have been Britain's oldest working weaver, Matthew Fowlds, a native of Fenwick, is pictured here working the loom in his home at Greystone Knowe in the east of the parish. He died a centenarian on 31 January 1907. His son George, after an apprenticeship with the tailors Stewart Bros. of Kilmarnock, emigrated to New Zealand in 1882 and founded what became a successful clothier's business in Auckland. He later entered politics and rose to become minister of education, which, coupled with his extensive work in the community, earned him a knighthood. Following his father's death, he shipped the loom to New Zealand and gifted it to Auckland Museum, where it is still on display. When Sir George died in 1934, his ashes were brought home and interred with his parents at Fenwick churchyard.

THE FENWICK CENTENARIAN
MR MATTHEW FOWLDS
AT HIS HOME
GREYSTONE KNOWE

C.F.K.

Pictured outside Greystone Knowe to commemorate his centenary on 22 May 1906, Matthew Fowlds stands with his thirty-six year old adopted daughter, Jeannie Cleland. To celebrate the occasion, a dinner for three hundred guests was held in the George Hotel, Kilmarnock. Fowlds' wife, Agnes Craig, whom he married in August 1846, had died three years earlier at the age of eighty-two. His grandfather had built the cottage on a half acre site on the Kilmarnock road to Grassyards Farm around 1778. Matthew was a descendent (five generations removed) of the Covenanter, Captain John Paton. After Matthew's death, Tom Handling occupied the cottage until the late 1950s, when it was left to fall to ruin, being completely demolished in 1970. In 1996, when Robert and Catherine McInnes retired from Grassyards Farm they built a new house on the site and now reside there.

This winter photograph of Laugh Fenwick was taken on Monday, 4 February 1907 as part of a series to commemorate the funeral of Matthew Fowlds who had died the previous Thursday. Following a brief service at Greystone Knowe, twenty carriages conveyed the mourners to the Orr Memorial Church for a further service where the congregation included the children of the village who were given a special holiday from school. Matthew was a member of this church all his days and was an elder for his last fifty years. From the church, the cortege wound its way up through the village to the cemetery where he was laid to rest with his late wife Agnes.

This 'Scotch Express' tricycle was one of many thousands built by the Howe Machine Company Ltd at their works in Bridgeton, Glasgow, from 1886 and through the 1890s. The rider is unidentified, but the bundles in his arm suggest a connection with the post office and it may be James Currie, Fenwick's postmaster, who died in 1936 at the age of 77. The Royal Mail experimented with tricycles from 1880, but initially it was found that most of its men were physically unfit to ride them. In 1895, however, sixty-seven tricycles (at £6 8s. each) had been purchased from Howe's for use by postmen throughout Britain, with a further one hundred being bought the following year. If postmen purchased their own, they were paid a weekly allowance of 4s. (20p). This innovation extended the free delivery of telegrams from a radius of three to five miles.

Lieutenant colonel William Reginald Houison-Craufurd and his wife Emily Maud, photographed by the bank of the loch on his estate at Craufurdland around 1900. The loch was man-made in the 1830s to supply the estate with fresh fish, mainly perch and pike, throughout wintertime when only salt meat was otherwise available. The oak tree behind them survives today. While the estate remains in the family's hands, Craufurdland Fishery has been open to anglers on daily permits since 1996, when it was dredged, cleaned and restocked with brown and rainbow trout. The winter of 1980 was the last to bring sufficient ice to allow curling, a favourite outdoor winter sport of the nineteenth century.

Hareshawmuir ('the moor of the deer wood') Lodge was built as a small shooting lodge for the Earl of Glasgow in the late nineteenth century. During the early twentieth century it was enlarged and extended on at least five separate occasions. The entrance tower was built around 1900 by Mr A.B. Paton (another descendent of the Covenanter, Captain John Paton), who had purchased it six years earlier. He also added the billiard room.

Two miles east of Fenwick the hamlet of Waterside straddles the A719, five miles north of Galston. This view from around 1904 looks north from the high ground to the south of Craufurdland Water which initially powered Alexander's carding and woollen mill. But for the mill, the hamlet would not exist. Between 1852 and 1916 it had its own post office which was situated in the buildings at the top of the row on the left; only the postbox survives. Primrose Bank, in the foreground right, was a Home Guard billet in the Second World War, but has since been demolished, while Willie Reid's joiner's shop, which peeks out to its right, is now a private residence. The hamlet's one-teacher school, Hareshaw Public (not pictured), was erected in 1828 under the patronage of the Earl of Glasgow and educated, amongst others, five doctors, three ministers and, in Sir George Fowlds, one New Zealand cabinet minister.